Is the
SPIRIT
of Man
ETERNAL

IS THE
SPIRIT
OF MAN
ETERNAL

SHIRLEY FORD HAYES

XULON PRESS

Xulon Press
2301 Lucien Way #415
Maitland, FL 32751
407.339.4217
www.xulonpress.com

Paperback ISBN-13: 978-1-6628-2364-0
Ebook ISBN-13: 978-1-6628-2365-7

DEDICATION

I dedicate this book to all those who want to know: What goes on in your inner man during conception, life, death, and the afterlife, and if your soul survives it all.

TABLE OF CONTENTS

All about Your Spirits from Creation to the Resurrection

Preface

God allowed me to go through a valley of tears; life left me broken. People walked out on me; I felt all alone. God placed me in His isolation chamber; He wanted me to heal and learn how to rely on Him. During this painful time, I discovered the function of the human spirit. Through much fasting and prayer, God connected with me in my heart. He does this to all whom He calls; He wanted me to become sensitive to his Spirit that I might know Him. I would love to share this incredible knowledge with you concerning the human spirit.

When we become one of his most trusted friends, he reveals knowledge with understanding and graces us with His miraculous power. It took many years to find the whys and why nots in this book. I have learned to recognize God and how to receive His favor. When I began to seek the Kingdom of God and His righteousness, He added prosperity to my life. Wealth is not always having lots of money; it is when you lack nothing. We need money, and I welcome it. I feel the presence of God with me in my daily walk and have reached that place of tranquility.

INTRODUCTION

Many people are ashamed to ask about their immortality, but they want to know. They suffer in silence, thinking others will judge them. They gather bits and pieces here and there, not being able to put it all together. Some even think to themselves, how does God speak to me and dwell in me? What are our purposes and the functionality of the genders? Why do we have the war between the sexes, and are women inferior to men? God wants us to know, and we have explored these areas over the years and found a way to break them down to you. I invite you to investigate the knowledge of the Word printed in this book; it will give you a vicarious experience into the mind of God.

CHAPTER 1

Before the celestial bodies were hanging in the galaxies, God was shining radiantly in His glory. He shines so brightly until no man can look upon Him (I Tim. 6:16). He is the center of our universe: things on the earth and in heaven could not exist without Him. Wherever God shows up, mighty works come forth. Therefore, Faith's men and women create an atmosphere of praise and worship to invite God into their presence. If God does not show up, miracles do not happen.

The Spirit of God moved across the waters to create the earth. His spoken words gave us a beautiful world. The earth brought forth grassy planes in the foothills beneath high mountains that extended into the blue skies. The forest provided green habitats for wildlife, and beautiful oceans multiplied with sea creatures. Great rivers branched out into mighty streams with beautiful flowers growing along its shores. The early sunrises and late sunsets shed light upon these views and bring praise to the creator.

What God has created is beautiful; He gave us a world of color filled with beautiful scenes. He added a backdrop of light that reflects upon His work and accents its beauty. Artists and freelance photographers have captured these scenes on canvases and pictures that are astounding. These men have captured moments that speak to us; they are our very thoughts without spoken expressions. These masterpieces are woven into our cultural fabric and are sold in art galleries or displayed in our museums. Men preserve these works, and nothing equates to where God has placed them in the universe.

God created man and woman at the same time: "So God created man in his image, in the image of God created he him; male and female created he them" (Gen. 1:27). The conception process of humanity took place in the mind of God when He said, "Let us make in our image, after our likeness" (Gen. 1:26). Humankind would become God's family. God would provide a home and the necessities needed for man to live on the earth. One of these provisions was a mate, but He had His reasons for delaying the process. God formed the world and all there in while He waited on the arrival of the man.

God gave birth to His idea when He formed Adam. The earth's creation gave the Lord much joy; His family was coming home. Occasionally, He would come down for fellowship with them; in return for His visit, His family would show their love and gratitude for Him through praise and worship. No man can render true worship without the Spirit of God, and no man can be in the likeness and image of God without his Spirit. Therefore, man had to be more than a body made of clay; since God is a Spirit, He and his family needed to be joined together by the same Spirit.

The next course of action separated the man from the beast of the field. God spoke to the earth, and it brought forth live animals out of the dust. God did not speak man into existence; He used His hands to gather dirt from the ground to make him unique from all other living creatures. He carefully formed the man's body down to the smallest detail. There was no material on the earth to make his spirit; only the supreme God could give life to a body made of clay. He did not call the four winds to breathe life into him (Ezek. 37:9), and neither did heaven send a rushing wind producing energy to activate life (Acts 2:2). Instead, God used direct contact; He injected Himself into the picture. God breathed His breath into the man's nostrils, and the man became a living soul (Gen. 2:7).

The dirt transformed into flesh. God's breath created the spirit inside man's body; this is the immaterial part of man that looks like

God. The same breath began the soul's conscious mind and quickly awakened the brain; his thought process was righteous and pure, just like God. Adam was a son of God; he was in the image and likeness of Him. His spirit recognized God; Adam was joined unto the Lord by his spirit. They became one (1 Cor. 6:17).

The man had a body, a soul, and a spirit (I Thess. 5:23). His body made it possible for him to live on the earth; this is the natural man. The soul, which is the mind, governs the body; today, God renews it by His Word. We have fellowship with God through our spirits; righteousness and everything good about man flows through it. The conscious mind and the spirit make up the spiritual man. God never breathed breath into any other creature on the earth. This spiritual body makes us different from all other aspects of God's creation.

God groomed Adam to dress the garden and name the animals. However, the excitement of his dream job soon wore off: There was no one to share his success with or talk to at the end of the day. He noticed all the animals had mates, but he grew sorrowful, seeing he had nobody like him. The Lord knew it was not good for him to be alone; this was the moment God was waiting on. He wanted Adam to realize he needed a companion to complete him.

Adam still loved and cared for the animals, but he desperately needed something more, He was like God; he had an intense compassion in his heart for love. This place laid dormant; there was an emptiness in his heart that the animals could not fill. Adam knew something was lacking; his spirit longed for her. He had never seen her face, but his soul was in search of her. God hears him and feels his pain. After all, "Who so ever finds a wife, find a good thing and obtain favor of the Lord" (Prov. 18:22). God would execute his plan for the institution of marriage between a man and a woman.

God did not go back to the drawing board to create the woman; when God created Adam, He also designed her in the blueprint. He pulled out the details and went into the formation process. His mind was on the creation's material aspect; God did not wish to form her from the dirt. He wanted to make her from something already made. He needed a rib from Adam so they would be one flesh. The woman would have a uniqueness that would be unlike the man and the other creatures. She would help Adam dress the garden, and her soft touch and kind voice would bring relaxation to him at the end of the day.

God caused a deep sleep to fall upon the man as he took a rib from his side. The Roman soldiers pierced Christ, the second Adam, in his side to bring forth a woman, too, the Church. The Lord fell asleep in death; both causes were for love. God made the woman and took her to the man. Adam's spirit was comforted; a righteous man's spirit will rest when he finds the right woman. Genuine love goes far beyond the flesh; it joins two souls together. Relationships joined together by the flesh will soon fall apart. He called her the woman; when a man calls you his woman, he needs nothing more. Adam was her source; she originated from the rib of the man. He would care for her and make her feel safe. The woman was intelligent, beautiful, strong, and virtuous, designed for the destiny God had purposed for them.

God took a bone from Adam that protected vital organs such as the heart, lungs, and other vessels to make the woman. The missing rib became Adam's weakness; it was still a part of him. The woman was close to his heart; Adam was sensitive to her pain. He became her protector; she became his most intimate companion and walked by his side. She loved, respected, and trusted him. A husband can protect his wife only if she is willing to submit to the rules that warrant her safety. Only a foolish woman would resist a mate like this. A man that exhibits these attributes is just a recipe for a happy marriage. But, of course, we are to submit to one another as well (Eph. 5:21).

After leaving Egypt, the Children of Israel; camped in the wilderness of Sinai. They accepted God's Proposal for marriage; the Lord wrote the marriage vows into a covenant of protection. God would be their protector, covering, and shield: "For thy maker is thine husband" (Isa. 54:5). The Children of Israel became the Lord's wife and Sarah submitted to Abraham and called him Lord; this title came from a different place in her heart. It went beyond a title of endearment or worldly status. Abraham was a righteous friend of God. His life and devotion as God's representative made him worthy of such high regard: "For the husband is the head of the wife, even as Christ is the head of the church: and he is the savior of the body" (Eph. 5:23). The proceeding clause after the word "Church" defines the term "head." The head is the savior of the body; the word "savior" means to protect, deliver from danger, or one who brings Salvation. Thus, the husband is a protector, and the wife submits to him as even unto the Lord.

God gave man and woman dominion over the earth before He created them; note; He uses the words, "let them have dominion" in the following verse: "And God said, let us make man in our image, after our likeness: and let them have dominion over the fish of the sea, and over the fowl of the air, and over the cattle, and over all the earth, and over every creeping thing that creeps upon the earth" (Gen. 1:26). God did not bless the union until He formed both the man and the woman: "And God blessed them, and God said unto them, Be fruitful, and multiply, and replenish the earth, and subdue it; and have dominion over the fish of the sea, and over the fowl of the air, and over every living thing that moves upon the earth" (Gen. 1:28).

The woman was in a leadership position beside her husband; they depended on each other to get the job done. The world was a perfect place with perfect people: these two people were like God. They were innocent children without sin. Adam had not argued with God about his excellent intention; he could not tell God how to rule the world. The woman would be part of the family; dominion over the earth would be a shared responsibility. Adam had no problem with this. Sometimes we must give up power to appease the heart; we cannot have it all. In doing so, you make someone happy besides yourself. Sharing is a necessary part of love; love is never selfish. When we spend time alone, we grow and understand who we are and what we need.

Jesus used different situations to give a teachable moment. Jesus taught one of the greatest lessons about manhood to His disciples.

The mother of James and John confronted Jesus. She went to Jesus and asked Him to Let her two sons sit beside Him in the kingdom, one on the left and the other on the right. The mother wanted her sons to lead in status positions; indeed, holding prominent positions of this nature would makes them great men. You will find the words of our Lord very inspiring, as he defines what makes a male become a real man.

Jesus told her that she did not know what she was asking. Were they able to drink the same cup as He? Were they able to be baptized of the same baptism as He was? Jesus told her they would indeed drink of the same cup and receive the same baptism. Jesus was not in charge of the seating arrangement; the decision was in His Father's hands (St. Matt. 20:20-24). High positions give people status; some people see your successes but fail to realize the hardship you faced and the sacrifices you made.

The other disciples became upset, but Jesus settled the dispute. He let them know that the Gentile princes, men that do not know God, exercise dominion over men. This behavior has no place among His people but allows the great person to be the younger one. The man that is the chief let him serve. He asked them, who was the greatest at the table, the man who sits, or the man who helps? Would not the man that sits at the table be greater: They know Jesus was the Messiah, yet He was the one who served. God does not want us to behave like the Gentiles who wished others to help them, but they should serve others in the spirit of love and humility. There is no place for this type of authority in the kingdom of God (St. Luke 22:25-30). Authentic manhood is about being a humble spirit with a heart to serve others. Jesus was our perfect role model; he was always a humble Spirit and willing to help.

Encoded in the heavens is a message of God that no man can erase. It is the most significant flow chart that expresses how the family should function as a team. Joseph, the son of Jacob, was called by God to save a nation. God used the solar system to show Joseph how his family would react to his commission. This lesson of observation included the sun, the moon, and the eleven stars. The survival of the human species depends upon these light forces; there would be no life on the earth without them. These lights are visible to us, and they both give us light and provide other properties.

These celestial bodies work together. The sun can outshine the moon anytime, but it goes down and allows the moon to come out: "And God made two great lights, the greater light to rule the day, and the lesser light to rule the night; he made the stars also" (Gen. 1:16). The conjunction "and" connects the sun and the moon in the verse; both are leaders and work side by side. The heat from the sun makes it unapproachable, and neither can we look at it with naked eyes. Everyone respects the sun; the heat can become intense at times. We benefit from the sun, but it can become a weapon against us. Some serious health problems can occur when we overexpose ourselves to its' rays. Neither the United States nor Russia has ever sent astronauts there. The sun is a force to be reckoned with; it is a replica of God. The sun symbolizes the Father's role in the family, who provides and protects.

The moon is equally as important, even though it is the lesser light to rule the night. The moon sets the mode for peace and calmness after an exhausting day; we unwind and hope for a brighter tomorrow. Some call the full moon the lover's moon because it is beautiful; this cannot be anyone else but the mother's role in the family. The rays are gentler than the sun, but we find it more appealing for rest and sleep. The moon is also nurturing and allows growth and productivity. Things seem to grow better overnight.

She welcomed the United States and Russia when they landed their spacecraft on her surface. Her kindness allows the stars to be awake with her. They are small, but they help her to produce light at night. The little stars lay in wait for the sun to rise each morning. Joseph said the sun, the moon, and the eleven stars would bow down to him, and they did when he became the governor of Egypt (Gen. 37:9-11). These celestial bodies represented his parents and his brothers.

There are also clues in the human anatomy that leads us to believe the husband is the protector. God designed their bodies differently and equipped them to function in their created capacity. Adam had a muscular body with broad shoulders to withstand rigorous work; he also needed physical strength to protect his family. Adam had the capabilities to father children and provided for them. God gave him intelligence; a courageous spirit to win battles, resolve conflict, make discoveries; and a mechanical inclination to invent things to improve life quality.

Eve's body was weaker than Adam's body; she engaged in less strenuous work. Nevertheless, God created her to be intelligent, industrious, and virtuous; these qualities define her values. She had the capabilities to give birth to children; God graced her with stamina and multitasking to meet the high demands of caring for a family. The continuous existence of society depended upon these two people; they worked together to bring about success on the earth.

CHAPTER 2

G od placed the Tree of Knowledge of Good and Evil in the garden. Some people feel that God should not have put the tree there, but love is never by force. He wanted humanity to love Him enough to choose Him. Joshua told the Children of Israel, "If it seemed evil unto you to serve the Lord, choose this day whom you will serve; whether the god which your father served that were on the other side of the flood or the gods of the Amorites, in whose land you dwell: but as for me and my house, we will serve the Lord," (Josh. 24:15). Joshua chose God; the freedom of choice is left up to us as well.

Satan is an evil spirit, and he got into the serpent to deceive man. The snake waited on the right opportunity to do it; the devil sowed deceptive thoughts into the couple's mind. He wanted them to doubt God and fall into unbelief. The devil planted the seed of distrust into their hearts, and if he could pull it off, he thought the creation would fail. Satan had deceived some of the angels in heaven to follow him the same way; it worked for him there, and indeed it would work now. He was a desperate man; he wanted them to become his followers.

The snake was very calm and cunning as he asked the first question:

> Yea, hath God said, Yea, shall not eat of every tree of the garden? The woman replied, but of the fruit of the tree in the middle of the garden, God had said ye should not eat of it, neither shall ye touch it, lest ye die. And the serpent said unto the woman, Ye shall not surely die. For God doth know that in the day ye eat thereof, then your eyes will come open, and ye shall be as gods, knowing good and evil.
> -Genesis 3:1-4-

The devil made them feel like they were missing out on something that God was withholding from them. They were already like God; they were in His image and likeness. If people are not cautious, they will buy into sales where beautiful things are popular and versatile.

She looked at the fruit and saw it was good for food, beautiful, and it would make one wise. The devil is a smooth salesman; she bought into his sales pitch. She reached up and touched the fruit. The woman ate the fruit and gave it to Adam, who stood beside her (Gen. 1:6). Adam was not at another location in the garden when she ate the fruit; he stood beside her. Adam was the protector; he failed to stop her. He made a split-second decision to violate the Law of God. They forfeited it all for what sounded like a better deal.

At that very moment, something happened in their spirits when they ate the unforbidden fruit. The Spirit of God left them; they felt the painful emotions left behind after sinning. When we violate the Laws of God, we grieve him. Our spirits morn within us, and there is the dreadful feeling of guilt and condemnation. Suddenly, their minds became conscious of good and evil; worldly knowledge replaced their innocence. Instantly, their eyes could judge between right and wrong; They had an oops moment when they realized that they were naked. Adam and Eve used their hands to cover their bodies. They ran for cover and made garments of fig leaves.

They ate the fruit and died a spiritual death; man's fellowship with God would be different. Their physical end, death, would gradually track them down. When we sin, there are consequences even though God will forgive us. Their souls were troubled and afraid of meeting God for fellowship. The pleasures of sin are short-lived, but the penalty can last an exceptionally long time. Adam and the woman knew they were in serious trouble; they needed time to process what had just happened. The couple bought this upon themselves; their anxiety levels were high. They knew the consequences would be damaging.

The act they just committed would affect their unborn children; yes, it was the will of God for them to procreate. When God blessed them in the garden, He also established the marital union and endowed it with children. All nations flowed from Adam and Eve, and each generation comes to the world as sinners: "Behold, I was formed in iniquity, and in sin did my mother conceive me" (Ps. 51:5). Their spirits were in darkness: "The spirit of man is the candle of the Lord, searching all the inward parts of the belly" (Prov. 20:27). Man would need restoration by the Spirit of God, the required candlelit. He would have a nature to sin and discern right from wrong; Man would eventually experience physical death.

Finally, God went to confront Adam in the garden; after all, things had gone wrong. God went directly to the source. He had been calling Adam for fellowship, and he was late showing up. When he did come, he was wearing a loincloth made of fig leaves. God could smell the stench of sin all over him. At this moment, the family fellowship was over; God became the Judge in the family court. Isn't it amazing how God can sniff out sin? Most women can mirror God in this respect; she can tell when things are not in place or how she left them.

God gave women great intuition since the fall in the garden. She searches out all the leading evidence, and notices change down to the minor details. She does not buy into things so quickly and examines them thoroughly before deciding. Sometimes women decide against an item in one store and look for something better, only to end back up at the first store to make a purchase. Most men hate going shopping with women because they take too long. Some fellows just grab things and go.

Even though Adam has never worn fig leaves before, the Lord did not address his new clothing right away. The relationship had already gone sour at this point, but God wanted to hear Adam's side of the story first. There is something about telling the truth that softens the blow even though it is hard to hear. Adam respected and valued God enough not to let anyone else tell Him what happened. Adam said, "I listened to your voice in the garden. I was afraid; because I was naked, and I hid" (Gen. 3:10). Some acts of sin make us ashamed because they expose us to others. These sins make you want to hide or get in a hole somewhere. We are open to criticisms, ridicule, laughter, and at last, the mercy of others. The world can be a cruel place, and we can tell who our real friends are in the time of trouble.

God wanted to know who told Adam he was naked and had he eaten of the forbidden tree. Adam stood before God wrapped in the evidence, a loincloth made of fig leaves. The conversation now went off the rails, but Adam knew how to make his case and keep a low tone in God's presence. First, Adam pointed out to God, "The woman whom you gave to be with me, she gave me of the tree, and I did eat" (Gen. 3:12). In other words, "Lord give me some slack; You are the one who made her for me." His actions seemed to have pointed out that he had been lonely in the garden, but he was doing all right until he met her." Lord, you gave her to me as my helper, and she prepared me a meal. I ate it." Adam placed the blame on the woman; he became a smooth attorney in a few hours. He did not indict the serpent. God did give him the woman to help, and she did get the meal for Adam. Adam confessed that he had eaten it.

The Lord looked at the woman dismissing her new fig leave dress that covered her nakedness. However, he asked her what she had done. The woman did not have the same law school experience as Adam; she presented her case very weakly as she nervously fumbled at the leaves on her new dress. She indicted the serpent by saying, "The serpent tricked me, and I did eat" (Gen. 3:13). She told on the snake. How was all this going to end? These two people and the serpent stood before God in judgment for their wrongdoings. God forgives, but there are always consequences when we sin. No matter how we present our cases before God. He is always fair. God was going to reward them according to their works.

The snake had a lot to say behind God's back; now, he had lost his voice. God looked on the snake and cursed him above all cattle and beasts of the field. The serpent walked; now, he would crawl on his belly and eat dust all the days of his life. The Lord said, "And I will put enmity between thee and the woman, and between thy seed and her seed, it would bruise thy head, and thy shall bruise his heel" (Gen. 3:15). There would be extreme hatred between the serpent and the woman. The devil hates a woman. She indicted him, and God would give her a seed to save all humanity and restore her status. God's favor would be restored to the woman one day, even though she would meet much opposition from biased and deceptive hearts.

We hear about the oppression of women through the news media. In Many places, women have no voice and little independence. Men gained the rulership over women by the Curse of the Law; most men have retired these old ways and love their wives as Christ loves the Church. They support them in their careers, help with chores at home, and assist in taking care of the children. Women in the United States have a supportive legal system and establish laws such as our Constitution that guarantee our civil rights and freedom of speech. We experience greater liberties as citizens than in some other countries. Many women hold public office in our government and help make our laws; we are among the world's most innovative and wealthiest countries.

The Lord greatly multiplied the woman's sorrow and conception; she would bring forth children in grief, and her desire would still be for her husband. The platform of the woman changed. They ruled together in the past, but now he will rule over her as she becomes dependent on him. She was no longer in a leadership position outside the home. The woman would perform domestic duties and care for the children. When God destroyed the world by water, Noah and his three sons were the only ones God commissioned. God upheld His Word; the husband would have rulership over his wife; "And God blessed Noah and his sons and said unto them be fruitful, and multiply, and replenish the earth" (Gen. 9:1). He said nothing to the women. Men took authority over the world. Eve brought this upon herself; God is just in whatever He does, and His Word is always right.

The Lord told Adam since he listened to his wife, he would curse the ground. In all the days of man's life, he would eat food grown from the earth. The land would bring forth thorns and thistles; thereon, it would need cultivation. Adam would earn a living by the sweat of his face; this was a task of hard labor and much toil. Adam's loss of innocence and his new nature to rule over his wife come into play. He did something different. God had already given him dominion over the earth; now, he had rulership over the woman. She lost her leadership position with him and took a step down. Adam claimed his rulership authority over her and named her Eve (Gen. 3:17-21).

The curse did not give man dominion over the woman; God does not give men control over people but animals. Authority means having complete control over an individual. Many marriages fall apart because some spouses want to control their mates. Dominion over people belongs to the sovereign God; in Him, we live, move, and have our existence (Acts 17:28). We can live in God and He in us, but we cannot live with someone that smothers us. People will run away from a relationship that will not allow them to grow. Rulership came about by the curse and ended at the Cross. Being a ruler has its advantages, but being a subject is not as enjoyable.

Man would now find his way back to God by Faith. The couple made a mistake; they were brokenhearted over it. They wished they could take it back and start all over. Adam still loved Eve, and he had not given up on her. Sometimes the thing that you love the most gives you the most trouble. God had not given up on her either; he knew she had a bad start, but there would be an excellent finish!

God would give her a seed to defend her honor; this seed would give the devil the final blow that brings him down forever.

God still loved them, and he slew an animal and made little coats of skin to cover them (Gen. 3:21). It must have been a difficult decision for a loving Father to send them out of their paradise. The Lord drove them from the garden to keep them from eating the Tree of Life. If they ate of the tree, it would cancel God's judgment upon them. The Tree of Life was the key to Adam's immortality; if he ate from the tree, He would never die. God places an angel at the garden entrance to keep them out (Gen. 3:22-24).

The Garden of Eden became a paradise lost to man. The Lord relocated the Tree of Life; it is in heaven (Rev. 22:2). Abraham looked for such a city: "By faith he sojourned in the land of promise, as in a strange country, dwelling in tabernacle with Isaac and Jacob, the heirs with him of the same promise; he looked for a city which has a foundation, whose builder and maker is God" (Heb. 11:9-10). The prophecy of the Lord shall stand; He would find favor with the woman again. The Virgin Mary would give birth to His Son, Jesus, to cover their shame. He will restore paradise to man through His grand plan of Salvation.

Sin affected the whole earth, vegetation, animal life, and even the atmosphere change. Adam made primitive tools to cultivate the land to grow food; keeping the pest and animals from raiding the garden would be challenging. God gave man dominion over the animals; most of them feared him; He still struggled to fight off the wild beast. It had never rained before, and even today, we experience different types of storms. Our government invests money into Global Warming and Climate Change. Men began to slay each other, Adam stayed clear of these corrupted men. Man lost the spiritual connection he had with God in the garden; somehow, he needed to appease him by some other means.

The door was wide open for different diseases to wreak havoc on man; his lifespan would gradually grow shorter and shorter. Humanity has always need God; presently, he needed him even more than before. Salvation was a long way ahead; his immortality will happen when God has subdued all things unto Himself at the end of time. All of this would come with a tall price, the precious blood of the Lamb. One day, the final enemy would stare a man in the face, Death; how would he go out to meet him?

Adam's sinful act gave the devil all the leverage he needed; the devil knew God told the man not to eat the forbidden fruit. Man disobeyed, and the penalty was death. God could not take back His Word. The devil held Adam and his seed as hostages; the sentence was the sacrifice of pure blood. What would God do; did He love brave enough to redeem him? Just one sin affected the whole earth; every man that comes into the world is born a sinner. His spirit needs Salvation. Man's spirit is like a candle; it requires God to light it.

CHAPTER 3

S in and wickedness grew mightily in the hearts of men; God was sorry that he made him. He sent Noah to preach, and the people rejected the message. So God sent a flood upon the earth. The survivors were Noah; his wife; his three sons, Japheth, Ham, and Shem; and their three wives. When the water on the earth dried up, Noah and his family left the ark and built an altar where they offered a sacrifice unto the Lord. They worshipped and gave thanks unto Him.

God responded to his people by making a covenant with them and animals. Yes, He loves the little animals too. God agreed to never destroy the entire earth again with water (Gen. 9:8-9). God knew most people would grow fearful in rainy weather; therefore, He placed the rainbow in the sky to confirm his agreement. We have many artificial bows, but none are as glorious as the rainbow. This magical arch with gleaming colors stretches across the heavens. We confirm that our God keeps his promises; He staged it where every man can look up and have trust in Him. We can only imagine the beauty of the Kingdom of God that lies beyond it.

God commissioned Noah and his three sons; this was His new order of business. God said nothing to the women. Before the flood, the woman was tasked with dominance to help the man to dominate the earth. Now the woman would provide care for the children and keep the home; she would depend on her husband to support her. God did not will it to be this way, but the sin in the garden brought this upon the world. After thousands of years of men ruling, it would not be easy for her to reclaim her position. Our only hope rested upon the death of Christ. When God sacrificed the animal to cover their nakedness, it also revealed our Redemption under Grace. God would save man and redeem him from the curse of the Law. God made up his mind to help humanity; He would send them a Redeeming Lamb to save His creation. He was setting things in motion; this would take some time.

God called Abraham to give birth to a people that would worship Him, and through his lineage, the Messiah would be born to save the world. He was a faithful and obedient servant of God; Abraham lived a long life and died at one hundred seventy-five. God's people struggled to find their way back to Him; they needed him in their lives. The Lord set the tone for worship in the garden when He killed an animal and made coats to cover them. Man not only needed outer garments, but he also required spiritual covering. The Children of Israel no longer shared the same family worship Adam had in the garden; he climbed high mountains to worship, just to be closer to the heavens where He dwells. Humanity offered up sacrifices by Faith that God would restore the fellowship with them.

There was a famine in Canaan; Abraham's Grandson, Jacob, and the Children of Israel ended up in Egypt. The children of Israel fell into slavery when a pharaoh inherited the throne that did not love them. They cried unto the Lord, and He heard them. Even in this, God was working to their advantage. Egypt was a wealthy place and a well-established civilization. God raised Moses to deliver His people out of Egypt. Pharaoh's daughter reared Moses; she found him in a basket floating near the Nile riverbank. His mother told his sister, Miriam, to place him there so the pharaoh would not kill him. The Israelites were multiplying too fast, and this put fear in the mind of the pharaoh. He commanded the midwives to kill the Hebrew baby boys to control the population. The Hebrews outnumbered the Egyptians; the pharaoh became disturbed about war, social unrest, and power shifting to the Hebrew nation.

Moses received one of Egypt's best educations; God prepared him to lead the Children of Israel out of Egypt and into their Promised Land. Moses ended up killing an Egyptian; he fled for his life and ended up in the house of Jethro, priest of Midian. God commissioned Moses on the backside of the desert through a burning bush. Moses went back to Egypt with his brother, Aaron, after spending forty years in Midian. He delivered the Children of Israel out of Egypt. The travel through the wilderness would prove to be a massive undertaking for Moses; he was in between pleasing God and troublesome people.

God was working on His plan of Redemption; even He smiled on the women. He called Miriam, the sister of Moses, to be a prophetess. She was a praise leader over the women's choir, and when they crossed the Red Sea, the women went out after her as they sang, danced, and played the timbrels (Gen. 15: 20-21). The Lord said, "I sent before thee Moses, Aaron, and Miriam" (Mic. 6:4). God sent a woman to lead with the men; this was a preview of God's plan for women in the Grace age. These three people were siblings of the same family. Today we have a kindred spirit; all Christians are family to Christ. Miriam's gift of telling God's plan, singing, dancing, and playing the timbrel in the camp brought encouragement to all.

Miriam was not just a leader over the women; she sang and ministered to the whole Congregation. The young women sang and uplifted all in the camp's spirits after the men went to battle and won. Moses gave them space to do so; he sang as well. It encourages a woman's spirit when men, especially her leader, support and recognize her Ministry's importance. Miriam's gift opened the door of success for her, but her character seemed to have closed it. She secretly conspired to turn Aaron against Moses when he married the Ethiopian woman.

The Lord smote her with leprosy and told Moses to put her out of the camp. Everything came to a standstill. Moses and the people were disappointed at her behavior. Her sin was grave; Moses still loved her and prayed for her restoration. God healed her and returned her to the Congregation. Once God calls you into the

Ministry, He does not take it back, but you can ruin your credibility. We never heard anything else about her, only that she died years later. Her bad seems to have outweighed her good; people do not put much emphasis on her Ministry. History notes Prophetess Miriam with men in the deliverance of the Children of Israel (Num. 12:1-16).

Moses valued the women's work; he allowed them to minister to all in songs, dance, and music. Moses was a confident and educated leader. The higher education institutions in Egypt were the ivy league schools of his time. Moses demonstrated excellent leadership skills and strategies. His apprenticeship under his father-in-law, Jethro, gave him the field experience to govern people. He could sing and lead; he led songs of victory in the choir during worship service. There was a lead chorus in the song where Miriam answered Moses back. He could share the Ministry with others, but he demanded order in the Congregation. Moses was committed to God; he did not tolerate foolishness in the camp of Israel.

God spoke to Moses on many occasions: "And the Lord said unto Moses, Lo, I come unto thee in a thick cloud, that the people may hear when I speak with thee and believe thee forever. And Moses said the words of the people unto the Lord" (Exod. 19:9). In the past, God developed a great relationship with other men and spoke to them. Abraham was one of those men; he was a humble and faithful friend. Now God was enjoying his relationship with Moses equally as well. These relationships reminded him of the fellowship he had with Adam in the garden and how special those times were.

God knew that man was fragile, but he was worth saving. When the Lord visited Adam, he did not see God. Instead, Adam felt His presence and heard His voice as he walked into the garden in the cool of the day (Gen. 3:8). Moses spoke to Him face to face; this means that God said to him through a cloud. These men were different from other men; their hearts, love, and devotion especially touched God. He knew these men were among His most obedient and trusted servants.

God loved His people; He led them by a pillar of fire by night and a cloud by day. Finally, God began to think things over; He knew their sorrows and saw their struggles. The Children of Israel lived in Egypt's culture and traditions for four hundred years; getting them back into the worship experience would be challenging. The Lord struggled with them as a man with an unfaithful wife, but He knew the second generation would find fellowship with Him. God counted the cost; He knew only a remnant would prove faithful through their works and obedience to Him. God desired to establish reliability, but just a few were all He needed to implement His plan.

Worshipping in the mountains finally paid off; this was where God wrote the Ten Commandments on two tables of stones and gave them to Moses. These laws were rehearsed repeatedly in the camp because they had not recorded the Word on scrolls. This set of rules became God's established Laws for His people. God finally decided to come down out of the mountains and fellowship with them again. He would dwell in an artificial tabernacle; the location would be in the center of the camp. God anointed artisans to do the work as Moses carried out the plans. The people would use the wealth brought out of Egypt to fund the construction. The Children of Israel were excited; this type of worship would bring everyman together into an assembly. The Levites and Aaron, the High Priest, would oversee the Tabernacle with Moses as their spokesman.

A good description of the completed Tabernacle tells us a wall was surrounding it. There was a front entrance that led into the courtyard. The brazen altar for sacrifice was the first piece of furniture in the yard, and secondly, the washbasin, where Aaron's sons sanctified themselves for their duties. The Tabernacle had one front entrance, which led into the Sanctuary. The table of showbread, the golden candlestick, and the golden altar of incense were the only pieces of furniture in the Holy Place. A veil or curtain separated another room behind the Holy Place; this room was the Most Holy place where the High Priest offered up the annual sacrifice. The Spirit of God would come down once a year and fill the temple. This ceremony took place on the Day of Atonement, and God would forgive the people for their sins.

No one entered the Tabernacle wearing shoes; the Sanctuary was sacred and Holy unto the Lord. The priests went into the Sanctuary daily to perform their duties, but only the High priest entered the Most Holy Place once a year. This room contained the ark of the covenant, which represented the Spirit of God. The High Priest took the sacrificial blood and sprinkled it on the mercy seat so God might forgive their sins. It resembled a chest with two handles on each end. Four priests were required to transport the ark; they could not move it by any other means. An angel was attached to each end of the ark, which overshadowed the top of the chest.

An unrighteous priest died if he entered the Most Holy Place; the priest had to live a worthy life before God. The people listened for his steps as he approached the mercy seat. He had a border around the bottom of his robe that made noise as he walked barefooted. The hem of his robe contained an alternate pattern of bells and pomegranates. They were happy if the bells kept ringing because their priest was still alive, making intercession for their souls. Today, every man has direct access to God; we can reach Him by Faith no matter where we are. The gift of the Holy Spirit gives us that connection we so desperately need; we worship Him in spirit and truth.

Let us revisit the golden candlestick, the only source of light mounted on a stand having seven lights. The seven lights represented the seven dispensations of time, time past, time present, and time to come, in which God provided Salvation for man. Aaron and his sons serviced the candlestick and incense altar that released a sweet fragrance over the temple. The brazen altar on the outside could never go out. The fire source at the Tabernacle was not human-made; upon its completion, fire fell from heaven and lit the altar. Aaron's sons, Nadab and Abihu, offer up strange fire on the altar; it was never to go out. God slew them (Lev. 10:1-2). Whenever Israel's children moved, the brazen altar coals were taken up and transported with them by the Levites.

The Tabernacle was just a means for the Spirit of God to dwell with His people; these things were signs and symbols of things to come. Jesus walked out of the shadow, fulfilling all righteousness. We are no longer working in the shadows of Him; we have become the sons of God and have tasted His saving Grace. Our immortality is guaranteed. We are just waiting for Him to glorify our bodies and reward us in paradise.

EVIL SPIRITS

CHAPTER 4

How did evil come about? It all began in heaven when God created the most beautiful angel named Lucifer. He was known as "the son of the morning," and he was good-looking, the very epitome of beauty. He dressed in the most precious stones: the sardius, topaz, diamond, beryl, onyx, jasper, sapphire, emerald, carbuncle, set and mounted on gold. He was anointed and ordained as a guardian angel. We believe he produced songs and music (Ezek. 28:13-19).

Heaven exists; God has given men of Faith a glimpse into the city. An underworld is lived in with the devil and unclean spirits; some righteous men can see into it. The devil can transform himself into the angel of light; he enters the lives of those who become false prophets and deceive many (2 Cor. 11:14). Native doctors spring up having familiar spirits; people visit them to harm others and wreak havoc on themselves. Sorcery is a bad idea; these practices boomerang. This action reminds me of sending a letter to the wrong address; the post office stamps it as a return to the sender. What you give out always comes back to you. Those that engage in black magic leave this world in terrible ways; the devil makes good on his agreements with them.

The Lucifer spirit lives in many Churches today; some people gifted in song and music are not humble. This spirit wants to lead all the choir songs; these folks even think choir practice is a waste of their time. I have seen some choir members take advantage of the pastor; his choir went to churches without his approval. People with humility are needed to build the body of Christ. I promise you, these people will give you a headache. Some people love attention; they will take over if you allow them to. The Church would become a concert hall if some followers had to decide what the Church's plan should be. A Church should have songs and music, but the Word of God is its foundation. When we lose the foundation, we have lost it all.

Music and songs are important; they set the mood for the environment. Sad songs move people to tears, while upbeats songs reduce the pain of loss. Sleep music relaxes the body, and we soon fall asleep. Music therapy brings relaxation to weary hearts. King Saul was troubled by an evil spirit; a wise servant suggested that a man who was a cunning player on the harp stand before King Saul and play. This player had to be intelligent and skillful; David was such a man. He was an anointed vessel of the Lord. When the evil spirit came upon King Saul, David played the harp, and the evil spirit departed from him (1 Sam. 16:14-23).

King David formed the first choir and orchestra. He was a musician and a songwriter who composed many works. David was an anointed vocalist; he sings the songs of Zion. David loved music and introduced the combination of music incorporated with worship. Sometimes the Spirit of God fell upon him; It moved him to dance mightily before the Lord. David sorts the very heart of God; when we practice what David did, we will experience the visitation of the Holy Spirit too. He gave us many beautiful and inspirational Psalms; they bring comfort to our hearts. He left them behind for us to enjoy, even though he did not write them all (2 Sam. 6:14).

Lucifer held one of the most promising positions in the garden of God; he was perfect in all his ways until wickedness was in him. He became lifted in pride when he saw his beauty and realized the power of his wisdom. This angel thought he was worthy of praise rather than praising someone else; he caused division among the angelic host and led a revolt against God. Pride caused him to inflate and exaggerate his value. He seemed to have forgotten God had all power; indeed, God could replace him with a humble and even more beautiful angel. Heaven could quickly go on without him.

God threw Lucifer and the angels that revolted against him out of heaven. He lost his position along with his beauty; he is no longer known as Lucifer. His name today is Satan, along with many others. Some of his fallen angels are bound in hell this day, and awful things would occur if they were let loose. Satan is the prince of this world; he lives in the atmosphere. He wants to win souls; he searches the earth for people to devour. Do not be deceived; Satan has power and is extraordinarily talented. He deceived Adam and Eve; if you are not careful, he will deceive you too. Satan has no respect for a person; he tried to trick Jesus after He fasted forty days. He wanted Jesus to fall and worship him; he will never outsmart God. The world is still under God's control, even Satan.

Jesus grew up and began His earthly Ministry; He taught, comforted, did miracles, raised the dead, and cast out demons. One day, Jesus and His disciples went to the country of the Gadarenes near Galilee. When Jesus left the ship and approached the shore, a raging wild man came walking toward Him naked; the man was in a pitiful condition. This man needed a bath, a haircut, a shave, and clothing; we can only imagine how awful he must have smelled. Some demon-possessed people stink. He had been in this condition for an exceptionally long time; the evil spirit drove him to make his home among the tombs of the dead.

The Gadarenes wanted to help him, and they devised a plan to catch him. They tried to restrain him with fetters and chains, but he grew powerful and broke out of them each time. No one could cast this evil spirit out of him; the people did not know what to do. Finally, the evil spirit drove him into the wilderness; people could hear him running in the mountains and tombs, crying and cutting himself. The blood ran down his body. Nobody could get close enough to treat his wounds; the devil had taken over his mind. Legion had a family that loved him, but his mental anguish made it impossible for him to live with them.

The Master had no fear of him; the devil had possessed his mind. Jesus saw him and felt his pain. Jesus had compassion on him; He left many behind and crossed the ocean to set him free. When the devil recognized Jesus, he fell on his knees and shouted, "What do you want with me, Jesus, Son of the Highest God? You cannot send me back to hell; it is not my time" (St. Mark 5:7). The devil knows how to stand on the Word of God, where we sometimes fail. Only one devil talked to God, even though his body contained many of them. One devil-possessed Legion; the others were his followers.

The Lord asked him what his name was. The man told him Legion. All the other demons began to talk; they did not want to go to hell. The Lord permitted them to go into the swine who were feeding in the mountains. When the demons entered the swine, they ran violently down a steep hill into the water and choked. Those standing nearby saw it and feared it; they ran into the city to tell it. When they returned to the site, Legion was clothed. He was sitting beside Jesus and in his right mind. Legion wanted to go with Jesus, but Jesus told him to go home and tell his family and others what the Lord had done for him. Legion went everywhere telling everybody; this became a mission for him (St. Mark 5:1-20).

The devil knows that there can only be one leader, and a house divided against itself cannot stand. Demons are subject unto their leader, and they support each other to strengthen the works of darkness. The devil uses the wicked man to orchestrates attacks on ministries by sowing bitterness and division to hinder the Church; this person wants to steal the Ministry. He has the Lucifer spirit and wants to be in control. If you play the silent game with him, this hidden enemy will continue to manipulate others to attack you. When you correct him on the spot, he becomes offended. He will leave and take others down with him. Sometimes you wonder why some men follow evil. People are often blind to the truth, while other times, they are doing evil themselves.

Some inexperienced people cannot identify the attacker; they go after the followers. Usually, when the head person cannot find anyone else fighting with you, they expose themselves and come out swinging. Locate the leader and beat him first, and the followers will go. Be cautious; this leader will go away and regroup. They will return with even more helpers to defeat you; they become stronger than before. A conspirator with his extra helpers cannot take you down. God will win the battle single-handed; He will fight the battle for you. Sometimes you do not see them anymore.

The devil must bind a man before he can possess him. He does this through wicked thoughts, ideas, and manipulation of situations that places the person under extreme mental pressure. Eventually, the person grows weak and gives in to the enemy; his thinking has become severely distorted. At this point, the devil takes over the mind and inhabits the body; this is what we call demon possession. People can willfully open the door for demons to enter their lives by engaging in wicked and ungodly activities. Satan and his fallen angels are spirits; they want to use the human body to advance their kingdom.

Some people think demon possession is when the devil passes through a man and becomes flesh; God will not allow this. Fallen angels have the power to do this, but God will have them chained in hell before they attempt. If the angels bound in hell were let loose, you would see some unbelievable things happening on the earth. God has ground rules, and the devil knows what they are. God will take care of us. Hell is the last place the devil wants to be bound; he wants to be free to roam the earth and win souls. He and his helpers are already convicted and await their judgment.

The mind and the body have a sinful nature; this makes it possible for the devil to inhabit them. The devil uses the flesh's works to tempt humanity to sin; the devil does not want the natural body; there is nothing good in it. The devil wants the same thing God wants from us: "our precious soul." These flesh sins are: The sexual sins are adultery, fornication, uncleanness, and lust. The sorcery sins are witchcraft and idolatry. The sins of anger are murder, envying, wrath, hatred, strife, variance, heresies, sedition, and emulation; the sins of incapacitation are drunkenness and reveling (Gal. 5:19-21).

A Christian cannot become demon-possessed. God and the devil cannot occupy the same house. The spirit is the part of man that produces righteous fruits unto the Lord: "But the fruit of the Spirit is love, joy, peace, longsuffering, gentleness. Goodness, faith, meekness, temperance: against such is no law" (Gal. 5:22-23). The spirit of man is God's habitation: "The spirit of man is the candle of the Lord, searching all the inward parts of the belly" (Prov. 20: 27). When we obtain Salvation, God lights that candle with His Spirit. We should always pray; our spiritual fire is never to go out.

> Warriors that are spiritually dressed can win the battle of darkness:
> Put on the whole armor of God that you might be able to stand against the wiles of the devil. For we wrestle not against flesh and blood, but principalities, against powers, against the rulers of the darkness of this world, against spiritual wickedness in high places. Wherefore takes unto you the whole armor of God that you may be able to withstand in the evil day and having done all, to stand. Stand therefore, having your loins girt about with truth, and having on the breastplate of righteousness; And your feet shod with the preparation of the Gospel of peace; Above all, taking the shield of Faith, wherewith you shall be able to quench all the fiery darts of the wicked. Saints, take the helmet of Salvation, and the sword of the spirit, and watching thereunto with all perseverance and supplication for all saints.
> -Ephesians 6:11-18

The children of God do not fear the devil: "Submit yourselves therefore to God, resist the devil, and he will flee from you" (James 4:7). It is impossible to resist the devil without submitting to the Lord. An undisciplined person has a long way to go before approaching Demonology. Jesus's disciples could not cast the demon out of a man's son; his Father took him to Jesus, who cast him out.

Later, the disciples returned to Jesus and asked why they could not do it. Jesus told them because of unbelief: He went on to say, "By Faith, we can speak to the mountain, and it will move into another place. Nothing shall be impossible to us if we believe; however, this demon only goes out by fasting and praying" (St. Matt. 17:14-23).

The devil loves a crowd, and if you give him an audience, he will perform. When the devil-possessed Legion, he drew attention to himself by causing the man to exhibit erratic behavior. Satan does not care who he hurts. He comes to kill, steal, and destroy. Many people wrongfully accuse the devil; some people believe he possesses all mentally ill people. The brain can become sick like any other part of the body. Some people inherit mental illness; it runs in their families, while others develop it through tragic experiences. Some people are weaker than others when letting go of unhealthy thoughts and handling severe pressure conditions.

Demonic spirits can attack you; the sons of Sceva and the priest took it upon themselves to cast out a demon. The possessed man told them he knew Jesus and Paul, but he asked who they were. The man who had the evil spirit jumped on them and wounded them; they fled the scene naked (Acts 19:13-15). Even the Bible tells us to lay hands suddenly on no man (1 Tim. 5:22). Someone can transfer the spirit of infirmity to another person. If you doubt, do not lay hands, but catch hands and pray—the prayer changes from the Laying on of Hands to the Prayer of Touch and Agreement. The Lord said the believers could cast out demons; the believer must be a true Christian.

Sickness occurs not because we have sinned, but these diseases came about by sin. Our elderly are afflicted with dementia and Alzheimer's. Sometimes these are our family members; they do not recognize you or remember who you are. They have moments of confusion and curse when you have never heard them use language like this before. You wonder if they are still a Christian, and it hurts to see this disease affect their minds. However, they are not responsible for this illness; our job is to be there for them. After all, they were there for us.

This disease attacked the brain and distorted their thinking; they do not realize what they are saying. The brain, the organ, is malfunctioning; the flesh has failed. Our Salvation preserves us unto the day of Redemption. If we live long enough, we will be grown up once and twice a child; we never know what will happen to us one day. They need our presence, our love, and genuine concern. Meet with their doctors and caregivers. Follow the instructions on their living will; make sound decisions concerning their health. Give them the love and respect they need, and in return, God will send an angel to help you in your time of need.

The elderly lose their independence as they grow frail; I was there for my mom. She recognized me until the day she died at ninety-seven years young. When her disease advanced, she gave me about two minutes of her time and drifted back into her little world. I spent quality time with her, even though sometimes she did not know I was there. I made sure she was cared for properly. I did her laundry at home and decorated her room for the holidays. I made sure she had clean, warm clothing and provided dinner for her on special occasions according to her diet. I visited her every week, and when I could not, I sent someone to check on her.

I listen to the dying; many have something to say worth hearing. Mother had a vision of heaven; God gave her a glimpse of the city. It was an open vision through her bedroom window; she tried to show it to me. I could not see it; Mother often spoke of angels. Two weeks before her death, she told me that she had something to share with me. I sat and listened. She said the Lord told her to hold on a bit longer; He was coming. Two weeks later, I visited her one Sunday evening after Church; she was eating chocolate pudding. Mom was enjoying it; she made me want some too. I enjoyed my visit with her, and about five hours later, God dispatched an angel to carry her home.

I saw her body before the mortician moved it to the funeral home. Her head was on her pillow, and her palms were up. Mom's spirit had left her body; I was not afraid of her. I checked to see if her muscles were relaxed or rigid when she transitioned; she was soft and warm. Instead, her powers were loose, and her position suggested that she surrendered unto the Lord. She was my mom. I held it together, but I hugged the corpse even as Joseph embraced Jacob's body in Egypt. Mom lived a good life; the Lord made her know that He was coming. God showed her the Holy City while she was at home with me; now, she is at home with the Lord.

I have many experiences with evil spirits that I encountered. I remember a deep heaviness that settled over the Church; it was a binding spirit where the people always seemed divided. It was challenging to deliver a message there, and I rebuked the evil nature of division under the Holy Spirit's anointing. The people grew quiet; the Lord was at work. I commanded it to leave. The Church was packed, and a lady was standing with a flare-tailed dress on the front pew. I felt the presence of something rush by me and make its way down the aisle past the lady with the flare-tailed dress. The lady felt something run past her too. She jumped away in fear, and the spirit left the building.

Simon used sorcery to bewitch the people of Samaria (Acts 8:9). Simon wanted to be great among the people of his community. When Philip the evangelist ran a revival there, the people turned to God. Simon wanted to buy the gift of Laying on of Hands with money; The disciples told Simon he had no part in the things of God. People that practice sorcery never have a good end. These practices open the door for demonic spirits to enter their lives. Sorcery is the work of the devil; nothing good comes from it.

I knew a man that practiced sorcery, and as he grew older, he heard things that nobody else could. He once heard horses running around his house squealing after midnight. He lived life his way; eventually, he started attending Church and got baptized in return for God to heal him. Unfortunately, the healing had not taken place; he quit attending the Church shortly afterward. The man went back to his old ways. He grew extraordinarily ill and went to the hospital. He prayed for a while, and he cursed for a time on his bed. You could smell him before you entered his room; this small detail lent itself to demon possession. The spirit of the devil would speak out of him;

he once said, "What are you coming for?" I read one of the healing scriptures, anointed him with oil, and prayed for him.

I had prayer with him before he died; his whole demeanor had changed. He was not cursing, and he was conscious of his environment. The man was calling on the name of the Lord. He was in so much pain; the doctor was getting ready to sedate him. The man still had a strong voice, and he was sending up a good prayer. I believe he knew God was willing to take him, but he seemed determined to go from the altar. I would have done the same. They took him to another floor for sedation on the elevator; in those days, the higher the floor, the sicker the patients were. The nurse returned and told us that something went out of his mouth and bounced across the elevator floor. I knew that God had done the work; the devil let go of him. When the devil releases some people, they vomit up things. He passed away peacefully a few days later.

I remember some visitors who brought an alcoholic to Church; the man was sick. I asked them to get him to the altar. They laid him on his back; something in his stomach moved up and down. We prayed and laid hands on him, and the movement left his body. He was terminally ill, but God allowed him to live. I also recall a lady that came to the altar and hopped up and down like a frog. I prayed and laid hands on her; the evil spirit left her. This evil spirit had just taken hold of her. The longer an evil spirit lives in you, the harder it is to cast him out. These spirits go out only by fasting, prayer, and laying on hands (St. Matt. 17:21).

The devil tried to kill my daughter; he knew God was going to use her in Ministry. She needed to travel to Charleston, South Carolina; God told me to pray for her before leaving. On the way to Charleston, a big mack truck took the front off the car. God left her in the car untouched, sitting in the driver's seat. She said to me, "Moma, I saw the truck and the trailer pass by my legs." The driver could not stop immediately; there was a braking distance. The driver ran back to the wreckage; my child was unharmed. It took a while for her to get over it. God is good.

THE OPERATIONS OF SPIRITUAL
GIFTS TAKES PLACE IN OUR SPIRITS

CHAPTER 5

Jesus sent Spiritual Gifts to the Church after leaving the earth. The Word of Wisdom, Word of Knowledge, Faith, Gift of Healing, Miracles, Prophecy, Discernment, and the Interpretation of Tongues are the Gifts of the Spirit. These gifts are expressions of God that comfort, encourage, and build up the Church. These gifts do not require an individual to hold an office (I Cor. 12:1-11). The Ministry Gifts are Apostles, Prophets, Evangelist, Pastors, and Teachers (Eph. 4:11). These gifts bring growth and structure to the Church; these callings require an individual to have an office.

We do not choose our gift. Some men ignore this fact and decide for themselves, but they regret it later. We do not have access to these gifts without God's approval; our spirits bring divine expressions and words of inspiration by the work of the Holy Spirit. Our gender does not determine who the recipients are; God decides where we best fit in the body. However, there seems to be an unclarity among men whom God will give them. Some believe that only men are suitable for the Ministry. This problem has led to division in churches, fallouts between friends, and even breakups in marriages; Religion is one of the social problems in the world.

Men have ruled the world for thousands of years; people do not accept change easily. These were the very thought of Apostle Paul when he said, "And this I say, that the Law, which was four hundred and thirty years later, cannot annul the covenant that was confirmed before by God in Christ, that it should make the promise of no effect" (Gal. 3:17). Those in the priesthood wanted to hold on to Judaism; Moses's Law could not cancel out God's covenant agreement with Abraham to bless him and his seed (Gen. 12:1-3). Some are comfortable with the way things are because they benefit from it, while others do not know or do not care. There is also a group with a preference for men over women; it seems like a competition between two sports teams. We will always have a small segment that believes God will use women in the Ministry.

Let us go back to the Garden of Eden. Perhaps, we can find an answer if we start from the beginning: "And God said, let us make man in our image, after our likeness: and let them have dominion over the fish of the sea, and over the fowl of the air, and the cattle, and over all the earth, and over every creeping thing that creeps upon the earth" (Gen. 1:26). This was God's original divine order for man on the earth. However, the man was the "head" of the wife, and she was to obey and submit to his protection. God ruled the man and the woman to have the power and dominion over the earth; God automatically placed the woman into leadership without controversy or dispute.

The Lord styled the Church after the marriage; here, we see "Christ" as the "head of His church." The "man is the woman's head"; woman is singular, which means his wife and no other woman (Eph. 5:23). We see the same order repeated as in the beginning. Saved men and wise men do not rule over their wives; they are in a relationship where they depend on one another. "Rulership" came about when man sinned in the garden; this was part of the Curse of the Law: "Wherefore the law was our schoolmaster to bring us unto Christ, that we might be righteous by Faith" (Gal. 3:24). Rulership was justifiable under the Law, but it ended at the Cross with the death of Christ.

Some people might say the Law was not binding when man sinned in the garden; God is an all-wise God. He knows the mind of man; He had a solution for this. He charged the sin in the Garden of Eden to the Cross: "Unto Adam also and to his wife did the Lord God make coats of skins and clothed them" (Gen. 3:21). God covered the nakedness of the man and the woman naturally. He also covered the man and the woman spiritually; the animal's slaying to furnish that covering foreshadowed the death of Jesus on the Cross. God protected us under His saving Grace.

Why did the woman need restoring beside the man? She lost her rulership position in the world when she sinned in the garden; her husband ruled over her and the world. The man went from headship to rulership: "Unto the woman he said, I will greatly multiply thy sorrow and thy conception; in sorrow, thou shalt bring forth children; and thy desire shall be to thy husband, and he shall rule over thee" (Gen. 3:16). Headship means the husband is the "protector" of his wife; rulership means to have "authority" and "control" over her. Neither men nor women like control over them; they are partners in the relationship and belong to each other (1 Cor. 7:4).

Noah and his family came out of the ark; they offered sacrifice unto the Lord. God destroyed the first world by water; God only commissioned Noah and his three sons. He left the women out of this order of business: "And God blessed Noah and his sons, and said unto them, Be fruitful, multiply, and replenish the earth" (Gen. 9:1). Is this the affirmation of God—she would take care of the home and children? Instead, the woman became dependent upon her husband to meet all her needs. Today, "Christ hath redeemed us from the curse of the law, being made a curse for us, cursed is every one that hangs on a tree" (Gal. 3:13). Today, women are free from this yoke of bondage. World War I released women into the workforce, the men went to war. Women today have the freedom to make choices concerning their lives.

God gave all hope through the seed of the woman. The Virgin Mary gave birth to Jesus; He died to redeem us from bondage under the Law. Suppose we return to the justification of the Law. In that case, we place ourselves under bondage again: "Stand fast therefore in the liberty wherewith Christ hath made us free and be not entangled again with the yoke of bondage" (Gal. 5:1). The death of Christ restored women into leadership and positioned them to help men rule the world; this is what the fight is all about. The woman knows her value; she is a son of God. All sons are entitled to their inheritance when their Fathers' die. she is reclaiming her position on the earth.

Many of our traditions are under scrutiny today because they are ingrained in our culture; some will never change. Our schools are beginning to do an overhaul on textbooks. Many years ago, the text showed leading jobs assigned to men only; now, they show women in these positions. Men also help with the chores around the house; young boys learn that it is alright for males to engage in these tasks too. Television programs show women in roles that were once predominantly held by men. we modeled them as our new normal. They are conditioning the younger generation to accept women in higher offices. These roles of women are changing in our society. We will face challenges, but modeling this behavior makes it easier to manage.

Women were forbidden to be taught the Torah, unlike their counterparts. They lived with their Fathers until they married, and if the Father died, the elder brother led them. The women could not earn a living as we do today; their families cared for them. Jesus could not choose women to be disciples, neither could Apostle Paul ordain women to the Ministry. These women were bound by thousands of years of culture and traditions. Women are slowly earning their way back; they are seeking what they have lost. They struggled through generations of people to get where they are now, and there is still much progress to be made.

Some blame it on the feminist movement, but they are seeking their rightful inheritance. Christ died and paid for it; now, women want to claim their position in the world. The era of the woman is here. Women do not want to leave their husbands, take men's jobs, neither compete with other men; they want acceptance and higher-paying jobs in the workplace. Women deserve equal pay for equal work, and women are up in the military, NASA space programs,

Congress, and our local government. Many hold positioners as governors, principals, college presidents, lawyers, doctors, and the clergy. It comes with Salvation. It is God at work; He is repositioning the woman.

Moses dealt with these same spirits in the wilderness. Zelophehad had five daughters and no male heirs; He died in the wilderness on their journey to the promised land. The daughters went before Moses and the priest and pleaded their case; they wanted what belonged to them even though it was not the Hebrew culture to give land to female children. They would not go away. The women did not wish to have their Father's legacy forgotten; their Father stood with Moses in all his disputes with the men in the camp. The daughter believed their Father's estate should not be taken from them; because they were not men.

Moses was a fair man; he inquired of the Lord. The Lord told Moses the women were right. God told Moses to make a law stating a man's daughters shall inherit his property if he died without sons. (Num. 27:1-11). Women are in the same situation today; they are the daughters of Zion. Jesus died and left them a natural and spiritual inheritance. This case is in the Lord's hand; He is saying yes! Yes! Oh yes! "The Spirit itself bears witness with our spirit, that we are the children of God. And if children, then heirs, heirs of God, and joint-heirs with Christ; if so be that we suffer with him, that we may also be honored together" (Rom. 8:16-17).

God uses our bodies, but the gifts are birthed and operated through our spirits. These spiritual gifts flow from the heart of God. The soul has no gender, no race, nor social class. God calls us to ministry from our spirits; In Christ Jesus, we are all the same (Gal. 3:27-28). Regardless of our gender, we become a son of God (Rom. 8:14). The conversation between God and us occurs in our spirits; God ministers to us through our souls. We are in a spiritual battle that cannot compete with carnal means. Jesus said, "I speak not of myself, but the Father that dwells in me; he does the works" (St. John 14:10).

Our greatest battle has constantly been overcoming the flesh. God does not want us to fight among ourselves; this brings about division in the body. God and the devil know that no good thing dwells in our flesh (Rom. 7:18). The meat wars against the spirit. We need to allow God to transform our minds with His Word to help us accept His plan. Neither God nor the devil wants the flesh; both want the soul of man. God is looking for that soul that will be a true Christian without being tarnished by the world. Being a Christian is not how we feel about things or having our way; it is about allowing the Word to conform us to the image of God.

Let us investigate what happens in your spirit when an individual preaches a sermon. When a person called by God performs, he starts most of the time alone; when the Holy Spirit manifests in his spirit, the magic happens. God joins in to help. At that moment, the anointing kicks in; he lifts his voice like a trumpet. The minister feels carefree, light, and highly intoxicated under the divine influence of the Holy Spirit. God keeps mounting him up into new heights into the heavenly realm; he soars with God in the Spirit. God, the preacher, is present on the scene. When the performer reaches the message's height, God slowly brings him down and leaves the performance. The performer can feel it in his spirit when God leaves, so he brings it to a close. If he does not close when God leaves, he will be going on without Him. The helper has come and gone. If this never happens, God has not called you.

People can tell when the anointing is present, even a blind man. They can feel it; they know when you are operating in the heavenly realm. Whether they are sinners or not, they connect with you and God through their spirits. God has opened their eyes; they, too, recognize the magic has happened. The Spirit of God has descended into the atmosphere. The floodgates of heaven spill over into the crowd, releasing God on the scene. The people are smiling with gratitude expressions on their faces, crying, and reaching out to God in tears. God is ministering to them; He is relieving them of their burdens. They got just what they needed. They reached out to God, and He reached back to them.

I believe God called Deborah to be the only woman judge over Israel because she was the best fit for the job. Her prophetic gift guided her in making decisions concerning God's people. She worked under a tree (Judg. 4:4); I often wondered why. Sometimes women minister in some unlikely places, but having the freedom and peace of mind to operate in your calling means everything. She was an unsung heroine; Deborah rode into the battle with Barak against the Canaanites. Barak is the only name mentioned in the Hall of Faith (Heb. 11:32). Mary ministered to the Savior in a stable filled with animals. Sometimes women ministries do not have all the bells and whistles others enjoy, but God perfects their Churches in time.

Apostle Paul is one of my favorite people in the Bible; I must build my argument around him. Paul, as well as Jesus, were in a Jewish society where someone placed controls on women. They wore clothes that thoroughly covered their bodies, and when they went into the street, they were seen and not heard. The women could not hold public office; they were unprepared. Jesus nor Apostle Paul could place them in an office; this was unheard of in the Jewish culture. The Elders did not teach the Torah to women; only men received this privilege. Women prophesied, but this was a gift and not a called office. Only Jewish men were scribes; they recorded the Word. Women supported and followed Jesus, such as Mary Magdalene; if they produced any works, the Bible does not contain them.

The Samaritan women experienced more freedom than the Jewish women; the Jewish people disassociated themselves from them. They were not pure-blooded Jews. God spoke to the Samaritan woman at the well; His words lifted her self-esteem and made her feel valued. The woman went into the streets and found Jesus an audience; no doubt these were her friends. This woman caught a glimpse of what Jesus could do; He would bridge the gap between their people. His message drew her in; she would never be the same again. The Lord fulfilled her vision when Evangelist Philip went to Samaria and preached to her people. Peter and John joined

Philip in the revival; Peter and John laid hands on the Samaritans, and they received the gift of the Holy Spirit (Acts 8:4-17).

Apostle Paul taught Priscilla and her husband Aquila; they carried the Gospel as a team. Paul was a graduate of the most prestigious school of his time; he was a high-class and caliber nobleman. This couple must have felt as if they floated on air; they had the best mentor of their time. They had a Church in their home and became fellow laborers with him. They heard a man named Apollos speak in Ephesus. He was an eloquent and influential speaker, but he needed reliable knowledge to deliver the Gospel's truth. Pricilla and Aquila took him home and taught him the Word (Acts 18:26). Priscilla, a female, usurped authority over a man; this is a valid point. This portion of Scripture violates other scriptures in the Bible.

Apostle Paul spoke to the Corinthians Church in public and replied, "But every woman that prayed or prophesied with her head uncovered dishonor her head" (1 Cor. 11:5). The women were up praying in public and prophesying: they were not quiet. It amazes me, women were prophesying in the Old Testament; why would God need to say: "And it shall come to pass in the last days, saith God, I will pour out of my Spirit upon all flesh, your sons and your daughters shall prophesy, and your young men shall see visions and your old men shall dream dreams" (Acts 2:17). The word "prophesy" in this text does not have the same meaning as in the Old Testament; God spoke about something different. This gift comes with a fresh anointing; it is manifested through the gift of the Holy Spirit and given by God to the individuals He chooses. Prophesy in this Scripture means to proclaim the Gospel, to preach.

The expression of God's glory is infinite; in the transformation, His credit goes from glory to glory (2 Cor. 3:18). He also restores things to their former glory, and when this happens, someone has errored. Judah went into captivity under King Nebuchadnezzar of the Babylonian Empire because they continually sinned against God. When the imprisonment was over, the Israelites returned to Jerusalem and reconstructed the temple. The ancient men, the priest, Levites, and chiefs of the fathers, wept; the temple had lost its former glory.

The young men born in captivity shouted with joy; they did not know the difference (Ezra 3:11-13). The Prophet Haggai delivered the message: "The glory of the latter house shall be greater than of the former, saith the Lord of hosts: and in this place will I give peace saith the Lord of hosts" (Hag. 2:9). On the day of Pentecost, God raised the temple in the hearts of man (Acts 1). God has transformed us into His image; we walk in the image and likeness of God, enjoying the fellowship of His Spirit again.

Men and women prophesied in the Old Testament; today is a new day. The divine utterance of God flows from the lips of the Daughters of Zion. How can this prophecy be different from what we have already heard? The Holy Spirit will stir up the gift in them; God will join them in their utterance. The sinner will listen to the Word; his conviction leads to repentance. God surprisingly slays him in the Spirit; the old man goes down, and a new man rises filled with the Holy Spirit: No man can preach alone; God does the work through his spirit. "We preach not ourselves, but Christ Jesus the Lord; and ourselves your servant for Jesus' sake" (2 Cor. 4:5). The woman has a message; she will preach it around the world before Jesus returns.

"God has chosen the weak things of the world to confound the things that are mighty, and the base things of the world and the things that are despised has God chosen, yea, and things which are not, to bring to nothing things that are: that no flesh should glory in his presence" (I Cor. 1:27). The woman is the weaker vessel; there is massive hatred between the woman and the devil. This mutual hatred has continued between the seed of the woman and the root of the devil. The woman's seed crushed the devil's head at Calvary, and Satan bruised his heel (Gen. 3:15).

In my conclusion, let us examine two passages of Scripture; Paul said, "Let the women learn in silence with all subjection. But I suffer not a woman to teach nor usurp authority over the man, but to be in silence" (I Tim. 2:11-12). The following Scripture is: "For God is not the author of confusion, but peace, as in all Churches of the saints. Let your women keep silent in the Church, for it is not permitted unto them to speak, but they are to be under obedience, as saith the Law. And if they learn anything, let them ask their husbands at home; for it is a shame for women to speak in church" (I Cor. 14:33-35).

What is the setting in this situation? Apostle Paul was conducting an important meeting. These women previously worshiped in the temple in separate courts from the men. The women were unlearned; they got lost in the conversation and became disruptive while asking questions. Apostle Paul needed silence without interruption; the business was most urgent. Paul did not have teachable moments; neither was it a time for learning. He stopped to correct the woman in love. It was a shame for God-fearing women to conduct themselves in such a manner. Apostle Paul told them to be quiet; their husbands would make them understand his message in private when they returned home. They were to display the same modest behavior under Grace as they did under the Law. The Law may change, but if we refuse to hold on to sound principles, we have lost the foundation of it all. People have taken this Scripture out of context.

We do not know the urgency of the meeting; we know that imminent dangers were imposed on him by unfaithful men and enemies of the Cross. The apostle met these challenges under pressure and triumphed as a hero of Faith. He desired to go home to be with the Lord, but the Saints needed him most. Paul said, "For I am in a strait betwixt two, having a desire to depart, and to be with Christ which is far better" (Phil. 1:23). Paul faced death countless times and said, "As it is said, For thy sake, we lose our lives all day long; we are as sheep for the slaughter" (Rom. 8:36). In later years, he became a martyr for Christ.

Apostle Paul was a wonderful person; he repositioned the woman back beside the man: "Nevertheless, neither is the man without the woman, neither the woman without the man, in the

Lord" (1 Cor. 11:11). Apostle Paul loved women. They became his fellow laborers. He meant the word "fellow" in every sense of the Word; She is a "son" of God. Women loved and supported him; some went to prison along with him. He listed Andronicus and Junia with the apostles (Rom. 16-7). The Book of Acts does not close out with an Amen; it remains open. The Acts of God will not close until the Gospel Crusade circles the globe. God is still acting and fulfilling His prophecy. Some people will receive Salvation during the tribulation, but they will suffer great hardships, even become martyrs for their Faith.

Apostle John wrote 2 John; he was the only apostle to grow incredibly old and die a natural death. Men seem to mellow out as they grow older, and I believe he needed to address a woman's book. In the Old Testament, we have Esther and Ruth; Apostle John manages the Elect Lady (2 John). Women gathered up people in their homes, and Elders resided over these services. Some hold the view that the Elect Lady is the Church; I believe her to be a woman who gathered up people in her home and became their pastor.

This woman was brilliant, dynamic, and wealthy; money answers all things. People treat you differently when you have money. However, money was not her best asset; she was eloquent, influential, and noble. Many of her attributes remind me of the Apostle Paul. This lady was highly spiritual and cared for the things of God. She had a beautiful congregation referred to as her children by John. He admired how the children were rooted in the truth; She demonstrated her faithfulness and skills to promote Christian growth. He encouraged her to continue in the Faith and to be aware of false teachers. This letter must have been encouraging to her, having it coming from one of God's very finest, Apostle John. God set His approval and blessings over the work through him; he compels her with all diligence to continue watching over the flock (2 John).

Some people wonder what the call of God is like; we all come from different backgrounds and have different experiences. The Apostle Paul experienced God's commission on his journey to Damascus. He was going to persecute Christian men and women and return them to Jerusalem. Apostle Paul was fighting the wrong people. He and his men set out on their journey. Paul came near Damascus, and suddenly a light from heaven shined around him. He fell from his beast onto the ground and heard a voice saying, "Saul, Saul, why persecutes thou me? And he said, Who art thou, Lord? And the Lord said, I am Jesus whom thou persecute: it is hard for thee to kick against the pricks" (Acts 9:4-5). He was converted and joined God's people. The Prophet Ezekiel experienced the Lord in a vision as an image of man: from his waist down; there was an appearance of fire, from his waist upward was the appearance of bright, glowing, hot metal (Ezek. 8:2).

I had a similar experience; God had been trying to get my attention for quite some time. I put Him off; I was hesitant about responding to His call. I thought the task was too complex; women preachers have a rough time on their missions. My procrastination led to some dire consequences; I went to the hospital to give birth to my last child. I suffered some complications that could have ended my life. The baby was not in a birthing position; I saw the fear on the doctor's face. He thought he was going to lose me. I had a prayer in my heart as he went up and brought the baby down.

God had me in His hands. I began to hemorrhage when the placenta, known as the afterbirth, broke into pieces. It was a wrestle for a while. Finally, the eight-pound baby girl was born beautiful and tired, and so was I. After resting up for a long time, the nurse brought the baby to me. I could not believe it was the same baby; she did not look the same. I thought to myself; *they brought me the wrong baby.* I thought to myself again; *the baby went through a rough time while giving birth.* I looked at the eyes as I examined her for further evidence. The eyes were a dead giveaway; I remembered her eyes being large and pretty. These were the same eyes, but the baby was even more beautiful.

I returned home from the hospital; I did not feel well. My body was telling me something was wrong, but I was young and strong. I prayed and asked God to help me; I thought everything would be alright. I went to sleep; I had a vision. It was not just another dream: it seemed so natural. I heard a noise and saw something that I could not identify off in the distance coming toward me. It had the appearance of a hot metal image radiating like the sun. I squeezed my eyes to get a better view; I tried to make out what it was. The light was too bright to look upon, and I realized this was God! I fell on my face; I could not stand in His presence. Fear gripped my heart, and I trembled.

God had a strong voice. He was angry at me, and He rebuked me. I felt His powerful presence around me. I was terrified, and He told me, "Go ye into all the world and preach the Gospel to every creature" (St. Mark 16:15). He commissioned me to minister to women and men; I fear God more than man. Yes, I got beat up many times on the field, but I survived all the attacks. God has always provided and protected me. He speaks in a little, still voice to those that are willing to listen; I met this God with the voice of a lion who can roar in His anger. Jesus is the Lion of Judah who dwells in unapproachable light; your "spirit" knows Him. I fell into the hands of an angry God; I have learned always to do what He tells me to do.

The Lord gave me some specific instruction to tell the Elder of the Church about my commission. He also said that I had given birth to my last child; He had work for me to do. When I awakened, I went to the bathroom. Something like beef liver passed from my body. I called my doctor, and he told me it was after birth. He thought he had gotten it all. However, when I went back to the doctor the following morning, healing had taken place.

When I returned to the Church, I told the Elder, and he suggested we wait to be sure. Patience is one of my most vital virtues, and I have learned to wait on God. I did not realize what the Elder was doing to me, but he worked in the wisdom of God. He would allow me to testify of the goodness of the Lord; a supernatural presence would come over me. He kept watching me. This presence got stronger and stronger; the people were moved by it even more. Then finally, he said, "You are an evangelist." The Elder had been testing me to be sure about the call.

He was an excellent mentor, and he made me earn everything the hard way. He said, "I got to make you tough; the field is much harder on women ministers." I was the only female minister to preach with four other males in the congregation. He was on the Ministerial Licensing Board; the Elder drilled me like a lawyer during the oral exam. I answered much more challenging questions than the male ministers. I went off to college, but what I gained from him cannot be found in a textbook. A woman must prove herself repeatedly. He trained me how to hold my own; I appreciate it now. The field is no place for crybabies but strong, experienced Christians.

CHAPTER 6

D o you remember the time you lost a
loved one? I am talking about a loss that changed your life.
You may have seen the physical evidence of death take hold of them
as the illness advanced into its final stage. The person slept more and
ate less. They saw things and believed people visited them that passed
on; we cannot relate to these things. Death for a believer is a time
of change; they seem to be between two worlds. A person in transition must let go of the earth that they might obtain the heavenly.

They are gradually passing through this life into the next. The
person may have undergone some pain along the way, but God takes
the sting out of death in the final moments. Death is the gateway of
escape into another world; we must strip off the flesh to go home
in the spirit. Flesh and blood cannot enter the city of God. The
citizens that live there are spiritual beings. Eventually, the pattern
of breathing changes as their body begins to shut down; at this
moment, we can track them to the chamber door of death. We
cannot enter in; they must go alone.

There is the Jordon River. I have visited a lot of terminally ill
patients before dying; they spoke of this river. Most of them had a
deep, grim fear of it; no natural man or unrighteous spirit can cross
over to the other side. Jesus, angels, and souls of just men who have
already passed over are waiting for them to come home. Why do
some people see this river? The Jordan River borders the land of

Canaan, which was the Promised Land of the Children of Israel. The Israelites had a grim fear of this river too. Joshua, Moses's predecessor, led the Israelites across this river with the priests and God's help. The same Spirit with Moses was with Joshua; God opened the Jordan up even as He opened the Red Sea for Moses. They went into their Promised Land; this was symbolic of heaven.

The dying process is a journey where we start letting go of the fleshly man, and the invisible world lays siege on our souls. The dying loses the five senses at death; the last sense to go is the hearing. So be careful what you say around them; they can hear you. Encouragement, love, and strength are what they need from us, not our tears, fears, and pity. The doctor, midwife, or a relative was there during their birth; likewise, they need to be surrounded and supported by solid and loving people during their transition.

I observed a sedated patient as she took her last breath. She was a plus-size woman with a large abdomen. A circular motion began in her lower abdomen as if it were gathering up something; it raised into her chest cavity as if something were releasing from the body. The nurse saw the patient had stopped breathing, and her heart had stopped. I do not believe brain activity dies immediately when the heart stops. It takes a few minutes longer; those that are conscious at this stage know that they are dying. Resuscitation always begins immediately after the heart stops; if the patient wills it so, the brain will die without oxygen.

The eternal spirit of man and the conscious mind leaves the body at death; this is the man that God wants to go home with Him. This man is in the image and likeness of Him. The brain is an organ; it connects and communicates messages to the rest of the body. It stores information like a computer; the brain is part of the body. When God breathed into Adam, He created the spirit inside the man's body already packaged with His Spirit. Something else also happened; the conscious mind formed inside the brain.

The mind is the data system that processes thoughts and reasoning. The reason is the soul of man; it is a part of the spirit. No one has ever seen the mind; an x-ray can photograph the brain, which is part of the body. Information from a computer can be wiped out and passed on to another computer system, just as at death, the conscious mind leaves the brain with man's spirit. God does not want us in heaven out of our minds. The heart and the conscious mind make up one spiritual man; God takes back home what He blew into him. The body is left behind for the family. The doctor knows when death has occurred; all the brain's clinical activity has ceased, and the heart has stopped. Finally, man has let go of the earth that he might obtain the heavenly; the angel escorts him to his long-desired home.

The believer is happy now; the Lord rejoices in the death of His saints. Most people put up a good fight to stay here, but they wrestle to no avail. Man's life is as vapor and a fleeting shadow. He let loose of the bands that lay hold on him. The old body aged; disease suffered it to perish; it grew fragile, frail, and feeble. Man's immortal spirit gets up out of the wreckage; he goes to God a spirit being, beautiful, strong, vibrant, and forever young. The man that escapes the body is angelic; he is not the exact reflection seen in the mirror (2 Cor. 4:16). I have talked to three patients who had out-of-body experiences throughout my life; the Lord reunited their spirits back into their bodies. The first man told me how peaceful it was to be out of the body; he did not want to return. The second man said he went to heaven and spoke of how beautiful it was; he did not wish to return. The third man went to heaven as well and saw family members singing in the heavenly choir. All three of the men were seasoned Christians. The first two were pastors, and the last one was a deacon.

The body goes to the funeral home for burial preparation; the spirit we loved has gone away. Death cannot conquer the love we have for them. We remember the good times and the sad times we shared while they were with us. Funerals are not for the dead; they are for the living. Humans grieve after the loss of a loved one. We need the comfort of our family and friends while we heal during this process. We celebrate the lives of the dead with flowers, cards, wakes, funerals, and repasts. The mortician embalms and dresses the body;

it is placed in a coffin, sometimes surrounded by flowers so family and friends can say their goodbyes.

The body seems to be in a deep sleep; life has gone out of it. Whether the body is cremated or buried in the grave, either way, it returns to the dust from which it was taken: "Then shall the dust return to the earth as it was, and the spirit shall return unto God who gave it" (Eccl. 12:7). The spirit leaves the body at death; I am glad that my conscious mind does not go into the grave: "Who knows the spirit of man that goes upward, and the spirit of the beast that goes downward to the earth" (Eccl. 3:21). Our spirit is like God; it cannot die. It goes to heaven to be in the presence of God, the saints, and the Angelic Host: "Whatever thy hands find to do, do it with thy might; for there is no work, nor device, nor knowledge, nor wisdom, in the grave, whither thou go" (Eccl. 9:10). The body sleeps, and there is no memory there.

Apostle Paul had an out-of-body experience; the church had a question about their immortality. He was able to share the divine mystery with them: "Therefore, we are always confident knowing that, while we are at home in the body, we are absent from the Lord: (For we walk by faith, not by sight). We are confident, I say, and willing rather be absent from the body, and to be present with the Lord, wherefore we labor, that, whether present or absent, we may be accepted of him" (2 Cor. 5:6-9). We get out of our bodies at death and go to God or, unfortunately, take up the resident in another location.

I had a near-death experience after having major surgery. The doctor told me I had a 50 percent chance of dying. After having the surgery, I went to the recovery room, and everything seemed to be going well; later, I was given a room out on the floor. The head nurse happened to be in the room; I grabbed her arm and told her that I could not breathe. I heard someone calling respiratory therapy over the hallway intercom. I thought this was the end; my three little children flashed across my mind. Their ages were seven, five, and two; who would take care of them? I lost consciousness, and when I came through, the doctor had reopened my neck. I was in shock; I could hear him talking as he tried to connect the blood vessel. I felt no pain, but I heard him saying, "I cannot connect it."

I had a prayer in my heart; I told the Lord, "Let my soul live, and it shall praise Thee." I claimed life over death: "I shall not die but live and declare the works of the Lord." Be careful what you say when people are in shock; they can hear you. The doctor went on to say, "I do not know anything else to do when people get like this but send them to the funeral home." God heard my cry. The doctor could not give up. He kept on working because life had not drained out of me. Finally, he said, "I got it." The blood vessel had broken loose in my neck and bled into my lungs. I was drowning in my blood, but God saved me. Of course, the doctor denied all these allegations when I repeated them to him before leaving the hospital.

After this episode in the room, they transported me from the room to the Intensive Care Unit. I grabbed a nurse's arm; I was twenty-eight years old, young, frightened, and alone. The incident happened so quickly, and my husband had just gone home. I told her not to leave me; she pulled a double and stayed with me all night long. Finally, the nurse returned to see me when I was better. She told me that she had a lot of respect for me, and she observed three tears roll down my face that night. The nurse had her first experience with a patient like me. She went on to tell me that her college professor informed her class this would occur with some patients. Somehow God connected her to me; she could not leave me alone. I needed the nurse's prayers and comfort that night; if death came, I did not want to die alone. The dying requires you. Do not fear them; all they need is your love, prayers, and comfort. Let them know that you are there.

I ended up in the Intensive Care Unit hooked up to all kinds of machines; a friend came to see me and broke down in front of me. They asked her to leave the room, and you could hear her crying as she walked down the hallway. The visitor was a young Christian; not being able to control her emotions made me feel worse. If you cannot be vital for a sick person, do not go. Neither do sick people need spectators; they need to be surrounded by family and friends that love them. They need your strength and prayers to see them through their difficult times. I had gone through a lot; I was an extremely sick woman. I prayed in my heart; I wanted to raise my little girls.

The devil was determined to kill me; later, I had another episode; they called a code blue. I had lost all my five senses except my hearing. I felt as if I weighed a thousand pounds, and my heart was the only part of me holding on to life. I knew my body was shutting down; I felt as if my spirit could leave my body at any time. I could hear and think, and I was not in any pain at all. I tried to see, but I could not. I sensed the medical staff around the bed, but the heaviness lifted off me after a while. God gave me another chance; He took me down to the gates of death and brought me back.

My eyesight returned to me, along with all the other senses. I looked around, and everyone was gone. I stayed in the hospital for about a month, but I went home. The hospital staff was happy for me; even one of the little cooks came down to see me off. He was peeping and smiling at me from the hallway. They all witnessed a miracle and played a vital part in my recovery; they were my angels. I thank God for all the front-line workers and the excellent services they render to all those in need.

My mom could only do so much; my dad was sick at home. He released her to come to take care of me for two weeks; my husband had to go to work. I needed someone to care for me; I was not strong enough to take care of myself. Mom was a strong Church Mother, and she knew how to pray. Mom could pray; I asked her how she learned to pray so well. She said the storms of life would teach you how to stay before the Lord until you have won the battle. She kept me encouraged; Mom has gone home now to be with the Lord. I miss her so much; she was a precious jewel. No matter how long you have had your parents, it does not seem like long enough. We would only be selfish to expect them to stay, especially when most of their days are in pain.

The doctor left the draining tube in my neck; I named it the bloody turtle. My two-year-old was not afraid of me; the two older ones seemed a little uncertain. She came to the bedside and pointed to what used to be an old sore on her leg. I worked hard to get that sore to heal; I even took her to the doctor. I never will forget it; she said while smiling, "The Lord healed my sore, and He is going to heal your sore too." I believed her. God has a way of encouraging us; we never know whom He will use to speak to us. Slowly but surely, I went back to work nine months later. My life had drastically changed. God blessed me with the job of my dreams. I went to work at my first mortgage company. I joined Corporate America; I caught the elevator every morning with my briefcase in my hand.

THE SPIRIT OF MAN IN THE
RESURRECTION AND HIS DESTINY

CHAPTER 7

—

We plant flowers in our yards or flower gardens with the hope they will spring up. Man's life is as a flower; it shares its beauty and fragrance with us. The flower soon fades and withers away. We sow it in God's flower garden with the hope it will rise one day. Some graveyards are beautiful, and others not so much. They all have one thing in common: the garden is sacred unto the Lord and us. We visit the cemetery occasionally to place flowers on their graves. We still love them; they have touched our lives and gone.

One day, God will resurrect the dead; this is our blessed hope. When Jesus died, His spirit left His body and went to hell. Jesus's final destiny was not in this place; He went there to preach and set the captive free. The body of Jesus's burial was in Joseph's new tomb. The same thing will happen to humanity; immediately after death, the spirit reaches its destiny. The bodies go down into the grave or cremated; either way, both end up ashes. I am glad the soul does not sleep with the body; it cannot die.

Before Christ died, everyone went to hell; it had two parts. Paradise or Abraham's Bosom was in the upper part of hell; this was the righteous resident. The lower part of hell was the place where all sinners went. It was a place of suffering. A great gulf separated the two parts; there was no way of escape. The spirits of the dead cannot come back to us. Lazarus, the beggar, went to Paradise, and the rich man went to the lower part of hell. Jesus took all the spirits of the saints out of hell back with Him when He went home. Today, when we die, our souls go immediately into the presence of God. Hell is still growing; people are going there every day.

Satan had the proper leverage to use against God; he was holding God to His words. God told Adam if he ate the forbidden fruit, he would die. Adam's violation of that law gave Satan the legal right to hold men hostage in hell. After all, God said He was righteous; He could not go back on His word. Satan knew if God saved humanity, it would take Him a while to come up with the ransom. God had a tall price to pay. Satan thought the man was hopeless, and his life was hanging in the balance. In the eyesight of Satan, the conviction was man's only option; his crime made him worthy of death. If God did not follow through, this was a clear win for him.

Satan knew the penalty was the blood of a Sacrificial Lamb; no natural animal sacrifice would do. Would this man become flesh like an ordinary man and die on the cross? Would He suffer the shame? Perhaps, Satan thought, "For scarcely for a righteous man will one die; yet peradventure for a good man some would even dare to die" (Rom. 5:7). We were God's most vital weakness. Our Passover Lamb died on the cross. Jesus cried, "It is finished" (St. John 19:30). Jesus paid the debt in full: "Blotting out the handwriting of ordinances that was against us, which was contrary to us, and took it out of the way nailing it to the cross" (Col. 2:14). Execution on the cross was not a noble way for a man to die; the beating made Jesus unrecognizable. He endured the agony and the shame because He loved us: "Greater love has no man than this, that a man lay down his life for his friends" (St. John 15:13).

An incident happened in school some years ago. I recall two young men who were the best of friends. One of the boys could swim, and the other could not. The young man that could not swim was determined to learn. Both slipped away from home and headed down to the country pond. They entered the shallow water; without a doubt, things got out of hand. The swimmer was not a skilled teacher; his friend began to drown. He panicked and began to fight the water. The swimmer did not have the necessary skills to save him; both ended up drowning. I believe he tried to rescue him, but the sure grip of death took them. He gave up his life trying to save his friend.

Jesus loved us the same; He gave His life for us. After leaving hell, His Spirit united with His body at the tomb. Jesus's body was perishable, but it was raised imperishable. It was sown in dishonor and raised in glory; it was buried in weakness and raised in power. It was sown a natural body and raised a spiritual body (1 Cor. 15:43-44). Now, Jesus was immortal with the capabilities to shine like the sky. He had a solid physical body that could be seen and touched; He could eat and fellowship with His disciples. Jesus could appear, disappear, and receive access to go anywhere; Jesus even walked through walls. When He ascended into the heavens, He stepped on a cloud and went home. He could defy the Law of Gravity.

I believe the Resurrection will happen in phases; Jesus was the first person to be resurrected. He became the first fruit of those who slept; He arose on the Feast of First Fruits (Lev. 23:8-14). The crucifixion took place in Jerusalem. After Jesus arose, the dead saints in Jerusalem arose and went into the city. I bet that was scary. They did not hang around long; Jesus took them back home with Him when He ascended (St. Matt. 27:52-53). Heaven is a far better place for the saints' spirits to be. It even gets better; we will enjoy a new heaven and a new earth in the future kingdom.

The Resurrection and the rapture are the same. When Christ raptures the Church, people will be going about their daily tasks. Two people will be asleep in bed; two women will be working at the mill. Two men will be working in the field; God will take one out of each of the three groups and leave one behind (St. Luke 17:34-36). There is one thing we know for sure; it will be business as usual. People will be engaging in left unattended activities; there will be many accidents and missing people. People will vanish into thin air.

I believe the rapture of the church will take place before the Tribulation: "Because thy has kept the word of my patience, I also will keep them from the hour of temptation, which shall come upon all the world, to try those that dwell upon the earth" (Rev. 3:10). The saints will meet him in the air:

> For if we believe that Jesus died and rose again, even so, them also which sleep in Jesus will God bring with him. For this, we say into you by the word of the Lord, that we which are alive and remain unto the coming of the Lord shall not prevent them which are asleep. For the Lord shall descend from heaven with a shout, with the voice of the archangel, and with the trump of God; and the dead in Christ shall rise first; then we which are alive and remain shall be caught up together with them in the clouds, to meet the Lord in the air: and so, shall we be ever with the Lord.
> -1 Thessalonians 4:14-17

When the Lord comes back for the church, He will meet them in the air. He will not come down to the earth. The Lord's grand entrance will take place after the Archangel blows his trumpet. Only the saints will see Him; no man can see His face and live (Exod. 33:20). Jesus's appearance in the air will be a private viewing for those going home with Him. Jesus returns with the spirits of all those that have gone to heaven; He reunites them with their glorified bodies. Some saints will be alive when Jesus comes back; God will transition them into their glorified bodies. All the saints will go up to the Lord in the air. Thus, we will escape the horror that will come upon the earth during the tribulation.

Some people will get saved during the tribulation, and many will die. God will resurrect them when He comes to set up His Millennial Kingdom. The Lord will come to the earth with all the saints; every eye shall see Him. Evil men will mourn because of Him. Every knee must bow, and every tongue must confess that Jesus Christ is Lord (Rev. 1:7). Jesus will establish a perfect society and will rule as the king of the earth. The Millennial Kingdom was the Jewish people's hope; they wanted to see Him rule as their king. God will give them their hearts' desires.

The Devil will be bound for one thousand years; when the thousand years are up, the Second Resurrection will occur. God will raise the sinner at this time. The graves, oceans, death, and hell will give up their dead. The Sinner will receive a new body; their bodies will be sensitive and durable for punishment. The Saints will receive a glorified body like Christ. Our spirits are immortal; they cannot die. All of us will live forever, but we will not share the same destiny. God will release the sinner from hell to stand before the Great White Throne of Judgement. A crown will be given to the Saints at the White Throne by God; it is their reward.

The Lake of Fire will contain death, the last enemy to be destroyed, and hell; this is the second death. Satan, his angels, the false prophets, and the sinners will go into the Lake of Fire. The earth burns with fire: "But the day of the Lord will come as a thief in the night; in the which, the heavens shall pass away with a great noise, and the elements shall melt with fervent heat, the earth also and the works that are therein shall burn" (II Pet. 3:10). The first heaven and the first earth will pass away; a new heaven and new earth will come down from heaven. God will now have subdued all things unto Himself. Man shall live forever in his glorified body with God; the immortal Spirit of man survives it all. **Amen.**

9 781662 823640